Changes in the Seasons

WRITTEN BY
Lucy Palituq

ILLUSTRATED BY
Lenny Lishchenko

When the seasons change, things all around us change, too. There are different seasonal changes in different parts of Nunavut.

Here are some changes that happen in each season in Clyde River.

In Clyde River, the land is brown and sandy in the summer. The flowers bloom. There are beautiful colours everywhere.

4

It starts to get warmer in the summer.
There is 24-hour sunlight. Summer insects
come to life.

Darkness returns at night in the early fall. It starts to get colder. Berries become ripe. Many people go berry picking.

Parts of the land become covered in snow in the fall. Plants on the land start to die.

The land is blanketed with snow in the winter.
The plants on the land disappear under snow.

There is not as much daylight in the winter. There are more blizzards. Hunters start to hunt mainly seal.

The daylight starts to become longer in the early spring. People are out more, enjoying the weather.

It starts to get warmer in the late spring.
Parts of the land start to melt.

Things around us are always changing. There are things to see and enjoy in every season.

About the Author

Lucy Palituq is from Clyde River, Nunavut. She and her husband, Mike Jaypoody, have three children: Carlos, Kim, and Ashevak. Lucy graduated from the Nunavut Teacher Education Program in Clyde River. She enjoys being outside with her children.

About the Illustrator

Lenny Lishchenko is not a boy. She is an illustrator, graphic designer, and comics maker, who will never give up the chance to draw a good birch tree. Ukrainian-born and Canadian-raised, she's interested in telling stories that people remember years later, in the early mornings, when everything is quiet and still. She is based in Toronto, Ontario.

Nunavummi